, 28130431

DATE DUE

DEMCO 128-8155

Hip-Hop World

Hip-Hop Fashion

by Sue Vander Hook

Consultant:
Emmett G. Price III, PhD
Chair, Department of African American Studies
Associate Professor of Music and African American Studies
Northeastern University
Boston, Massachusetts

CAPSTONE PRESS
a capstone imprint

J 746.9
VAN

Books published by Capstone Press are manufactured with paper containing at least 10 percent post-consumer waste.

Library of Congress Cataloging-in-Publication Data
Vander Hook, Sue, 1949–
    Hip-hop fashion/ by Sue Vander Hook.
    p. cm. — (Velocity. Hip-hop world.)
    Includes bibliographical references and index.
    Summary: "Describes the fashion of hip-hop, including its history, designers, and style icons" — Provided by publisher.
    ISBN 978-1-4296-4017-6 (library binding)
    1. Fashion — Juvenile literature. 2. Hip-hop — Juvenile literature. 3. Rap (Music) — History and criticism — Juvenile literature. 4. Hip-hop — Influence — Juvenile literature. I. Title. II. Series.
TT515.V36 2010
746.9'2 — dc22   2009028166

APPLE $21.99

Editorial Credits
Megan Peterson, editor; Ashlee Suker, designer; Marcie Spence, media researcher;
    Eric Manske, production specialist

Photo Credits
Alamy/PYMCA, 6; Brian Chase/123RF, 15 (top); Capstone Studio/Karon Dubke, 13, 14 (all), 16 (top and bottom), 20, 41; CORBIS/Atsuko Tanaka, cover; DVIC/Howard R. Hollem, 22 (top); Getty Images Inc./Al Pereira/Michael Oachs Archives, 19, 26; Getty Images Inc./Florian Moser/Stock4B, 9; Getty Images Inc./Frederick M. Brown, 31; Getty Images Inc./Gautam Narang, 29; Getty Images Inc./Michael Ochs Archives, 36, 39, 40; Getty Images Inc./Scott Gries, 18 (bottom), 33; iStockphoto/ andyjibb, 28; iStockphoto/Xsandra, 8; Jeffrey Banke/123RF, 23; Landov LLC/Ron Wolfson, 25 (bottom); Newscom, 22 (bottom), 27 (bottom), 34; Newscom/AFP Photo/Timothy A. Clary, 44; Newscom/KMazur/WireImage, 45; Newscom/PNP/WENN, 27 (top); Newscom/UPI/Ezio Petersen, 32; Newscom/UPI Photo/Laura Cavanaugh, 12; Newscom/WENN/Jody Cortes, 43; Newscom/ WENN/Ken McCoy, 35; Olga Savchenko/123RF, 15 (bottom); Shutterstock/Alexander Kalina, 7 (pink belt); Shutterstock/alias (old wall background throughout); Shutterstock/averole (splash element throughout); Shutterstock/ayakovlevdotcom, 5 (dancer), 21 (top); Shutterstock/Cyriel, 21 (bottom left); Shutterstock/dendong, 7 (coat); Shutterstock/Dooley Productions, 37; Shutterstock/Elke Dennis, 10; Shutterstock/Idigital, 18 (top); Shutterstock/James Steidl, 42; Shutterstock/JJJ, 11; Shutterstock/John A. Anderson, 5 (graffiti); Shutterstock/kolosigor, 16–17; Shutterstock/lev radin, 4; Shutterstock/Lucian Coman, 25 (top); Shutterstock/MAT, 24; Shutterstock/Meliksetyan Marianna, 7 (legs); Shutterstock/ pandapaw, 38 ; Shutterstock/Petrov Stanislav Eduardovich (cement wall background throughout); Shutterstock/Pokaz (black banner element throughout); Shutterstock/Sergey Peterman, 7 (orange belt); Shutterstock/WilleeCole, 21 (bottom right)

The publisher does not endorse any products whose logos may appear on objects in images in this book.

The author would like to thank her daughter Jalene Vander Hook for her valuable contributions to this book.

TABLE OF CONTENTS

How It Began

Shoes with fat laces. Oversized hoodies. Jeans that hang low. Hip-hop fashion wasn't created in a designer's studio. In the 1970s, it began on the streets of the Bronx, a New York City **borough**. This was a time when hardship and unemployment gave birth to art, music, and dance.

FASHION IN THE BIG APPLE

New York City has been a fashion hot spot for many years. Fashion Week, New York's most important fashion event, kicked off in 1993. Each year, designers from around the world flock to Fashion Week to show off their lines.

In 2006, the Museum of the City of New York honored hip-hop fashion. The exhibit, called Black Style Now, featured clothing worn by Diddy, Lil' Kim, and LL Cool J.

Young people who lived in this mostly African-American and Latino borough expressed themselves in many ways. Graffiti artists painted on buildings and train cars. MCs wrote rhyming lyrics to pump up the crowds at street parties. Breakdancers spun on their heads to the beat of the street-corner DJ. No matter how they expressed themselves, hip-hoppers used fashion to stand out from the crowd.

borough one of the five divisions of New York City

Hip-hoppers in the 1970s dressed in whatever they had. Some breakers danced in sweatpants and T-shirts, while others danced in nylon tracksuits. MCs wore tight jeans and bomber jackets.

By the 1980s, rappers like Kurtis Blow and Big Daddy Kane had become hip-hop royalty. They added custom-designed suits, heavy gold chain necklaces, and multi-finger rings to their look. The more **bling** they wore, the more successful they appeared.

bling ⟫ *flashy jewelry sometimes worn to show wealth*

CHIC MEETS HIP-HOP

In September 1991, a Chanel fashion runway show in New York City was a mix of chic and hip-hop. Models strutted down the catwalk in flowing chiffon dresses. But they also wore big gold chains, wide flashy belts, fishnet stockings, and black leather jackets. The event was a benefit to raise money for disadvantaged New York teens.

As hip-hop became more popular, people wanted to be part of it. Millions wanted the music, but they also wanted the look. The styles that began on the streets developed into a multibillion dollar fashion industry.

CHAPTER 1

Clothing & Footwear

Hip-hop styles began with inner-city youth. They wanted to stand out, so they wore what no one else was wearing. A one-of-a-kind outfit drew praise and boosted the wearer's confidence.

JEANS HANGIN' LOW

Jeans have always been a staple of the hip-hop look. In the 1970s and 1980s, slim-fitting jeans were popular with both men and women. Some DJ and graffiti crews painted their names down the legs of their jeans.

Levi Strauss & Co. invented denim blue jeans in 1873.

In the 1990s, baggy jeans replaced slim jeans in many hip-hoppers' closets. The jeans hung down around the hips with no belt. Prison-issue pants were often too big and fell down around the hips. Because belts could be used as a weapon, prisoners weren't allowed to have them to hold up their pants. Some hip-hoppers copied the prison look to appear tough. They bought the best dark denim jeans they could afford in sizes two or three sizes too big.

In the 2000s, hip-hop jeans that were fitted around the waist with wide legs gained popularity with men. Rocawear, a fashion line started by rapper Jay-Z, and Diddy's Sean John brand offered this jean style. Women's jeans became fitted with slim legs.

T-Shirts & Hoodies

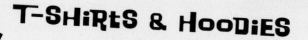

T-shirts were standard hip-hop fashion from the start. Some were airbrushed with graffiti-inspired art. In the late 1980s, rap group Public Enemy talked about social and political topics in their songs. Soon, T-shirts were printed with strong social messages and **rebellious** statements. And then there were hip-hoppers who preferred tank-style undershirts. They often paired these shirts with matching T-shirts.

The early 1990s saw hip-hop T-shirts go bright and bold. Los Angeles clothing company Cross Colours came out with baggy T-shirts in bright colors. Hip-hop group Kris Kross made the clothing famous in the video for their 1992 song "Jump." Female rap and R&B group TLC also sported Cross Colours T-shirts.

Hip-hop T-shirts crossed over into the **preppy** look in the late 1990s. Polo shirts in bright colors such as blue, yellow, and even pink became popular. Today, rappers such as T.I. and Kanye West wear the preppy look in their music videos and on the red carpet.

In 1994, Snoop Dogg appeared on *Saturday Night Live* wearing a Tommy Hilfiger sweatshirt. The next day, the sweatshirt sold out of stores throughout New York.

Hip-hoppers began sporting huge hooded sweatshirts and sports jerseys in the 1990s. Eminem put on an oversized hoodie and low-riding sweatpants to create the look he is still known for. In the 2000s, designers punched up the hoodie look with bright colors and all-over prints.

rebellious ⟩⟩ disobedience to the people in charge

preppy ⟩⟩ *a style of dress made up of classic clothing and a neat appearance*

WHATEVER Suits You

Breakdancers, also called b-boys and b-girls, danced in nylon tracksuits back in the 1970s and 1980s. The slippery material helped them twirl and slide.

By the mid-1980s, MCs and DJs caught the tracksuit bug. Rap group Run-DMC favored the Adidas tracksuit. Velour tracksuits became popular near the end of the decade.

Jay-Z

As rap music became more successful in the 1990s and 2000s, the hip-hop look changed. Rappers like the Notorious B.I.G. and Jay-Z wanted a more high-class image. They often dressed in expensive suits.

TiME FOR JACKETS

In the 1970s and 1980s, hip-hoppers walked the streets in jackets made of sheepskin, leather, denim, and fur. Many rappers, DJs, and graffiti artists painted their crew names on the backs of their jackets. Today, down jackets, leather coats, cropped jackets, and even fur coats are still popular in hip-hop fashion.

A GOOD SPORT

The Starter brand jackets were first made for professional sports teams like the Raiders and the Bulls. But they later became popular hip-hop attire.

1971 — The Starter company is founded in New Haven, Connecticut.

1980s — Starter brand clothing line partners with major-league sports teams to make team jackets and caps.

1991 — The film *Boyz N the Hood* comes out, starring rapper Ice Cube. The movie features Starter clothing, which helps make the brand more popular with hip-hop fans.

Late 1990s — The popularity of Starter jackets fades.

2009 — Starter pays the Dallas Cowboys quarterback Tony Romo to help make the brand more popular.

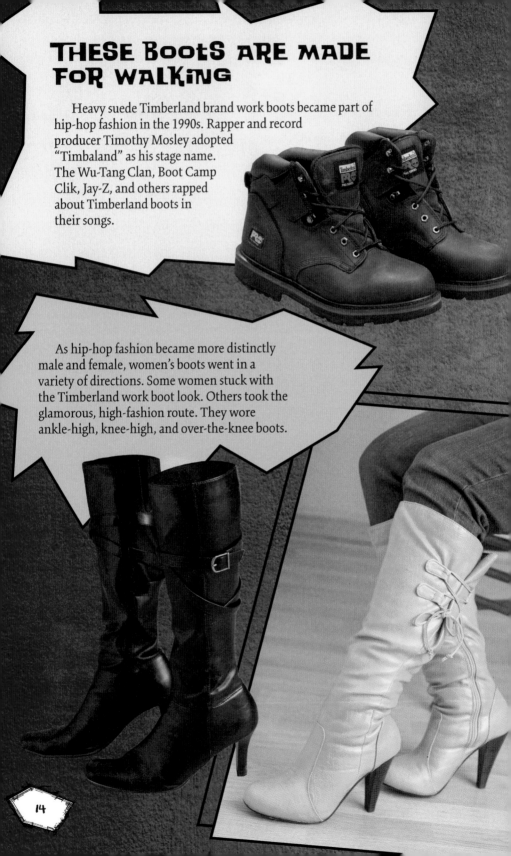

THESE Boots ARE MADE FOR WALKING

Heavy suede Timberland brand work boots became part of hip-hop fashion in the 1990s. Rapper and record producer Timothy Mosley adopted "Timbaland" as his stage name. The Wu-Tang Clan, Boot Camp Clik, Jay-Z, and others rapped about Timberland boots in their songs.

As hip-hop fashion became more distinctly male and female, women's boots went in a variety of directions. Some women stuck with the Timberland work boot look. Others took the glamorous, high-fashion route. They wore ankle-high, knee-high, and over-the-knee boots.

StiLEttoS

One of the favorite shoe and boot styles of female hip-hoppers is stilettos. Stilettos have high, thin heels. Heel height can range from 3 inches (7.6 centimeters) to more than 6 inches (15 centimeters). They make legs look long and strong.

Late 1500s — Heeled shoes first appear in Western Europe.

Late 1600s — King Louis XIV of France wears red heels. Only French royalty are allowed to wear red heels.

1950s — Stilettos become all the rage. The styles of French designer Robert Vivier are very popular. The *Daily Telegraph* newspaper reports on a stiletto heel that is 3.5 inches (9 centimeters) high. These high-heeled shoes have metal shafts in the heels.

Mid-1960s — As flats become more common, the stiletto's popularity fades.

1970s — Designer Manolo Blahnik reintroduces the stiletto design.

1990s — The popularity of stilettos is revived by rappers such as Lil' Kim and Foxy Brown.

2000s — Stilettos are a fashion must-have.

CRAZY ABOUT SNEAKERS

Even more important than boots in hop-hop fashion are sneakers. B-boys and b-girls started wearing sneakers in the 1970s and 1980s. Clean white shoes proved that a breaker had skills. Only "bad" dancers scuffed their sneakers.

Soon the sneaker trend caught on with other New York City teens. Popular sneaker brands in the 1980s included Nike, Converse All Stars, Pro-Keds, Adidas, and Pumas. Because some kids couldn't afford more than one pair, cleanliness became key. Kids used toothbrushes to keep their sneakers looking new. Others painted their old shoes to make them look new again.

Time to change up the look of a sneaker? No problem. Hip-hoppers used wide laces to match the color of their hats and T-shirts. Ironing these "phat" laces helped make them even wider.

Some hip-hoppers left the laces out of their shoes. They were copying the prison look. Prisoners weren't allowed to have shoelaces.

The sneaker craze spread beyond New York City to the rest of the country in the mid-1980s. Nike released its popular red and black Air Jordan sneaker in 1985. Basketball superstar Michael Jordan wore them in every game. Air Jordans first became popular with rappers, who passed the style onto their fans.

Today, custom-designed sneakers are popular in hip-hop fashion. Some artists paint one-of-a-kind shoes for their customers. They paint anything from family members to movie posters on the shoes.

In the early 1980s, the National Basketball Association (NBA) didn't allow red or black sneakers. They fined Michael Jordan each time he played in a pair of Air Jordans.

HiP-HoP HitS MTV

In the 1970s and 1980s, kids living in big cities like New York and Los Angeles grew up around hip-hop culture. They listened to the music and copied the hip-hop fashions they saw every day. But kids living in small towns and rural areas didn't hear or see much hip-hop.

All that changed when *Yo! MTV Raps* debuted on MTV in 1988. *Yo!* helped spread hip-hop music and fashion to small towns across America. The program was hosted by Andre "Doctor Dre" Brown, James "Ed Lover" Roberts, and Fred "Fab 5 Freddy" Braithwaite. It was MTV's first hip-hop music show. America's youth liked the music. They also wanted to copy the hip-hop styles they saw on TV. Hip-hop fashion was no longer just an inner-city trend. It was for anyone.

Ed Lover

Fab 5 Freddy

Doctor Dre

Yo! MTV FaSHioN

» Members of the rap group Run-DMC hosted the pilot episode of *Yo! MTV Raps*. They wore black fedora hats, gold chains, black shirts, and dark jeans.

» Female rap group Salt-N-Pepa appeared on the show's first episode. They wore gold jewelry and acid wash jeans.

A Bit of Africa

In the late 1980s, rappers such as Queen Latifah, A Tribe Called Quest, and De La Soul added African traditions to their styles. They used fashion to show they were proud of their African heritage. These African styles included shirts and hats made of kente cloth. The clothing was often red, black, and green. These are the colors of many African flags.

Queen Latifah

Hats, Hair, & Bling

Hip-hoppers are always fashion forward with their accessories. They often top off their look with a hat, a fresh new hairdo, or a shiny piece of bling.

>> Kangol hat

HiP-HoP HatS

In the 1980s, Kangol hats were all the rage with hip-hoppers. Rappers like Run-DMC and LL Cool J wore Kangol hats. Slick Rick even formed a rap group called the Kangol Crew. One member of the rap group U.T.F.O. had so many Kangol hats that he was called the Kangol Kid.

Baseball caps have been popular with sports fans for decades. But rappers made them into hip-hop style in the 1990s. They wore them tilted, turned to the side, and backward.

In the 1990s and 2000s, some rappers added fedora hats to their looks. Rappers like Jay-Z, the Notorious B.I.G., and LL Cool J sported these broad-brimmed felt hats.

SPORTING A DO-RAG

For hundreds of years, people have wrapped cloth, called do-rags, around their heads. At first, do-rags served a purpose. Some farmers and other laborers used do-rags to soak up sweat during hard labor. In World War II (1939–1945), women working in factories used do-rags to keep their hair out of the machinery. African-Americans stretched do-rags over their heads to create waves in their hair or to keep their cornrows in place.

Tupac's Bandana
In the early 1990s, Tupac Shakur sported a bandana wrapped around his head and tied in front.

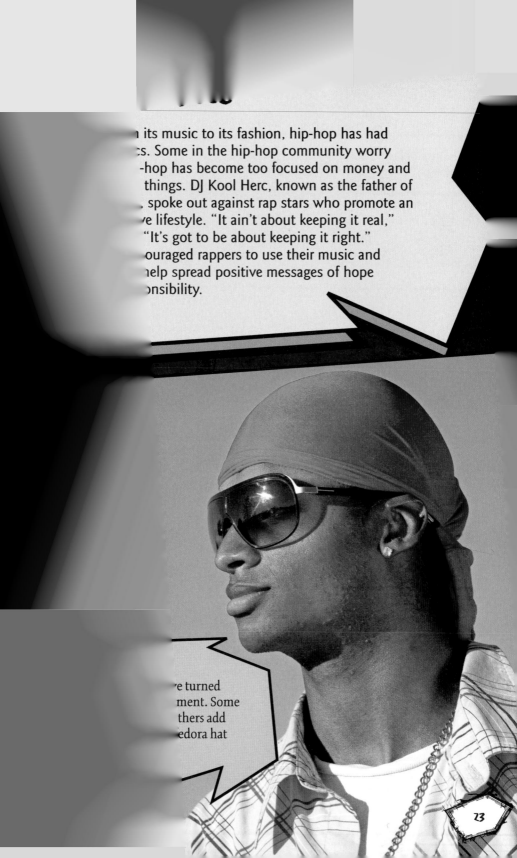

its music to its fashion, hip-hop has had
s. Some in the hip-hop community worry
-hop has become too focused on money and
things. DJ Kool Herc, known as the father of
spoke out against rap stars who promote an
e lifestyle. "It ain't about keeping it real,"
"It's got to be about keeping it right."
ouraged rappers to use their music and
help spread positive messages of hope
onsibility.

e turned
ment. Some
thers add
edora hat

FASHION HAIR

Hairstyles have always been important in the hip-hop community. From afros to dreadlocks, hip-hoppers turn heads by rocking these stylish 'dos.

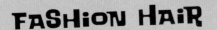

» **cornrows** — hair braided in rows very close to the scalp

trendsetters — ODB and Method Man of Wu-Tang Clan, Snoop Dogg

» **hair weaves** — long strips of hair; the hair can be glued to the scalp, sewn into, or braided into the natural hair.

trendsetters — Lil' Kim, Da Brat

» **shaved head**

trendsetters — LL Cool J, Rakim

CORNROW ART

Actress Cicely Tyson made cornrows popular on her TV series *East Side/West Side* in 1963. The style remained a favorite among African-Americans throughout the 1970s.

By the 1990s, hip-hoppers began making cornrows into an art form. The variety of designs ranges from simple straight braids to spiral patterns. Cornrow styles can take hours to complete. But with the right care, the hairstyle can last a month or more.

» dreadlocks — ropelike strands of hair formed by matting or braiding the hair

trendsetters — Lauryn Hill, Lil Wayne

» afro — tight curls styled in an evenly rounded shape

trendsetters —Ice Cube, Questlove

» jheri curls — glossy, loose curls

trendsetters — Easy-E, Kurtis Blow

» caesar — short hair with a fringe of bangs over the forehead

trendsetters — Eminem, Ludacris

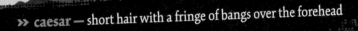

» hi-top fade — a tall afro with the sides cut very short; a hi-top fade that leans to one side is called "the gumby."

trendsetters — Fresh Prince, Kid 'n Play, Big Daddy Kane, Tupac Shakur

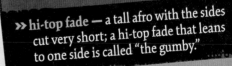

Fresh Prince

ROCKIN' tHE BLING

The bling look began with long, heavy gold chains in the 1980s. Rappers Kurtis Blow, Big Daddy Kane, and Run-DMC helped make these chains a staple of hip-hop fashion.

Big Daddy Kane

By the 1990s, hip-hoppers added flashy pendants to their chains. These huge diamond-studded plates often spelled out a person's name. Even belt buckles got a kick of bling. They sometimes displayed names in gold, **platinum**, or even diamonds.

platinum ➤➤ *a very valuable silver-white metal often used in jewelry*

WORLD'S BIGGEST BLING

Rapper Lil Jon's "Crunk Ain't Dead" pendant is the largest diamond pendant in the world. It was added to the Guinness World Records in 2007.

Weight: 5 pounds (2.3 kilograms)

Height: 7.5 inches (19 centimeters)

Width: 6 inches (15 centimeters)

Number of diamonds: 3,756

Cost: $500,000

GRiLLZ

Gold and jewels moved to the teeth in the 1980s. They were called grillz. The most expensive grillz were inlaid with precious jewels. Rappers like Flavor Flav, Big Daddy Kane, and Kool G. Rap were among the first to add grillz to their looks. By the 2000s, Lil' Flip, T-Pain, and Nelly helped turn grillz into a fashion statement as well as a status symbol.

Flavor Flav

EARRINGS, BRACELETS, & RINGS

Huge hooped earrings, called doorknockers, became a favorite with female hip-hoppers in the 1980s. Rappers like Roxanne Shante and Salt-N-Pepa helped make these oversized heavy gold hoops popular. But although the earrings were big, they weren't always made of real gold or diamonds.

CELEBRITY BLING

Where do the hip-hop stars buy their bling? One of the hottest hip-hop jewelry stores is Jacob & Co. in New York City. The store began as a small booth. In the mid-1990s, singer Faith Evans recommended the store to her husband, the Notorious B.I.G. Soon other rap stars began wearing the jewelry. Today, celebs like Diddy, 50 Cent, Madonna, Beyoncé, and Justin Timberlake sport bling from Jacob & Co.

What's That Bling?
The term "bling" started in the southern United States. In the late 1990s, Southern rappers Lil Wayne and B.G. sang about bling in their hits "Millionaire Dream" and "Bling Bling." In 2003, the word was included in the Oxford Dictionary. In 2006, the word was added to Merriam-Webster's.

Heading into the 1990s, hip-hop bling moved to the wrists, fingers, and hips. Thick gold bracelets, rings, jeweled belts, and gold chains around the hips became hip-hop hits. Big, colorful sunglasses embedded with jewels were popular with men and women. Some hip-hoppers added diamond piercings to their fashion statements.

3

Selling the Look

As the hip-hop look spread, some fashion designers and rap artists started clothing lines. They based their fashions on everyday hip-hop styles.

KARL KANI

In 1989, Karl Kani became the first fashion designer to make hip-hop clothing available to the general public. His oversized jeans were popular with hip-hoppers. They no longer had to buy their jeans two or three sizes too big.

TIME FOR KARL KANI

1989 — Karl Kani opens his first store on Crenshaw Boulevard in Los Angeles, California.

1991 — Rapper Dr. Dre helps promote the brand.

1999 — The Karl Kani collection is shown at the White House to President Bill Clinton and Vice President Al Gore.

2001 — Karl Kani launches Kani Ladies, a fashion line for women.

2002 — Karl Kani wins the Urban Fashion Pioneer Award at the Urban Fashion Awards in New York.

Karl Kani

The key to Kani's success was getting the right people to wear his clothes. He outfitted Tupac Shakur, the Notorious B.I.G., Snoop Dogg, and the Fresh Prince. People saw what these stars were wearing and wanted the same look. Wearing Karl Kani clothes became a sign of success. In just two months, Kani's business exploded. He went from shipping a few thousand pieces of clothing a month to 3 million items a month. He became known as the "Ralph Lauren of the streets."

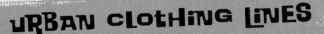

URBAN CLOTHING LINES

Other designers were quick to catch on and start their own hip-hop lines. They brought hip-hop style to people from all walks of life.

>> **1992 — Phat Farm** Russell Simmons, cofounder of Def Jam Records, starts Phat Farm clothing for men. The mixture of urban and preppy catches on. He later expands the line by adding Baby Phat, a clothing line for women.

>> **1992 — FUBU**
Daymond John founds FUBU, a clothing line made for and by African-Americans. FUBU means "For Us, By Us."

>> **1998 — Sean John**
Founded by rapper Sean "Diddy" Combs, Sean John is one of the top-selling hip-hop lines for men. In 2004, Diddy wins the Council of Fashion Designers of America's award for Menswear Designer of the Year.

» **2004 — Respect M.E.**
Missy Elliott partners with Adidas to release her Respect M.E. fashion line for women. The line includes sneakers, tracksuits, jackets, and T-shirts.

» **2003 — Apple Bottoms** Rapper Cornell "Nelly" Haynes establishes Apple Bottoms, a popular hip-hop fashion line for women. Celebs such as Fergie, Ashanti, and Oprah wear the brand.

» **1999 — Rocawear** Shawn "Jay-Z" Carter and business partner Damon Dash start an urban clothing brand called Rocawear. The line caters to both men and women. Rocawear becomes one of the top-selling hip-hop fashion lines.

To the Rest of the World

Hip-hop designers and clothing companies didn't hesitate to market their styles worldwide. They shipped to other countries and sold their fashions online. Anyone in the world could then dress hip-hop. People in Japan especially took hold of hip-hop fashion. Japanese designers created their own hip-hop fashion lines.

In 2004, Japanese fashion designer Nigo, right, teamed up with rapper and producer Pharrell Williams, left, to launch the hip-hop fashion line Billionaire Boys Club.

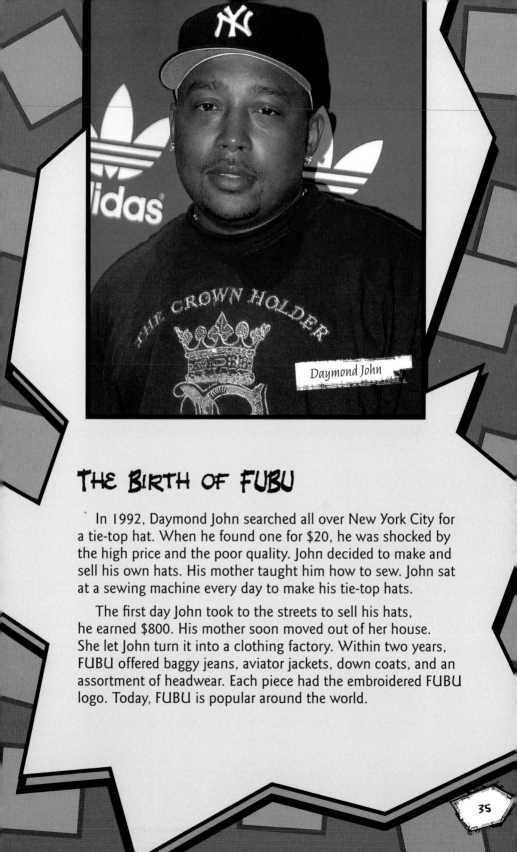

Daymond John

THE BIRTH OF FUBU

In 1992, Daymond John searched all over New York City for a tie-top hat. When he found one for $20, he was shocked by the high price and the poor quality. John decided to make and sell his own hats. His mother taught him how to sew. John sat at a sewing machine every day to make his tie-top hats.

The first day John took to the streets to sell his hats, he earned $800. His mother soon moved out of her house. She let John turn it into a clothing factory. Within two years, FUBU offered baggy jeans, aviator jackets, down coats, and an assortment of headwear. Each piece had the embroidered FUBU logo. Today, FUBU is popular around the world.

Style Stars

LL Cool J

LL Cool J burst onto the hip-hop scene in 1985 with his hit single "I Can't Live Without My Radio." LL, whose nickname stands for "Ladies love Cool James," has maintained a successful hip-hop career for more than 20 years. Whether it's a beret, fedora, or do-rag, LL is rarely seen without a hat.

LL Cool J was the first celebrity to help sell the FUBU brand.

LL launched his clothing line, Todd Smith, in 2006. His collection features graphic hoodies and T-shirts for men.

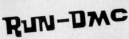

RUN-DMC

Run-DMC changed the face of hip-hop music with the 1983 singles "It's Like That" and "Sucker MCs." Many rappers of the early 1980s used funk and disco styles in their songs. Run-DMC scaled back their sound to just drums and a **turntable**. The group's hard-hitting look was just as powerful as its new sound.

In 1986, Run-DMC gave a shout out to their favorite sneaker in the song "My Adidas." After the song's release, Adidas Superstars sales skyrocketed. That fall, Adidas executives attended a Run-DMC concert. When the band played "My Adidas," thousands of fans held up their Adidas shoes. Adidas soon paid Run-DMC $1 million to **endorse** their sneakers.

turntable ⟩⟩⟩ *a circular, revolving surface used for playing phonograph records*

endorse ⟩⟩⟩ *to sponsor a product by appearing in advertisements*

>> heavy gold chains

>> black Kangol and fedora hats

Joseph "Run" Simmons

>> black Cazal eyeglasses

Jason "Jam Master Jay" Mizell

>> black jackets and pants in denim and leather

Darryl "DMC" McDaniels

>> shell-toe Adidas Superstars with no laces

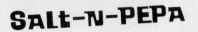

Salt-N-Pepa

Salt-N-Pepa entered the rap scene in 1985 with the single "The Show Stopper." After selling more than 8 million albums, Salt-N-Pepa is considered the greatest female rap group of all time. They changed female hip-hop fashion from rough and tough to glitzy and revealing.

» asymmetrical haircuts

» braided gold chains

» doorknocker earrings

Cheryl "Salt" James

Sandy "Pepa" Denton

Dee Dee "DJ Spinderella" Roper

» tight-fitting acid wash jeans

1980s FASHiON

The 1990s saw Salt-N-Pepa sporting black floppy hats and polka-dot tops. They wowed fans while wearing hot pants, cut-off denim shorts, and Lycra body suits.

1993 album

Entertainment Weekly magazine listed the 1980s fashion of Salt-N-Pepa as one of the 50 Pop-Culture Moments That Rocked Fashion.

asymmetrical	a shape that cannot be divided so both pieces match exactly in shape and size

EARLY FEMALE MCs

The first female rappers wore a mix of tough and glitzy fashions. They wanted to look strong in a male-dominated industry. But they also celebrated being female by adding bling and showy fashions to their looks.

» **Sha-Rock** was the first female MC to be part of a well-known crew. She started out as part of the rap group the Funky 4 + 1. In 1981, they were the first rap group to appear on *Saturday Night Live*. Sha-Rock wore a mix of plain black clothing, wild stripes, and bright colors.

» **Roxanne Shante** came on the scene in 1985 with her hit single "Roxanne's Revenge." Shante's style included gold doorknocker earrings, leather jackets, and even boxing gloves.

» **MC Lyte** began rapping at the age of 12. In 1986, she released her first single "I Cram to Understand U." MC Lyte sported a denim jacket, huge gold chains, doorknocker earrings, and rings on every finger.

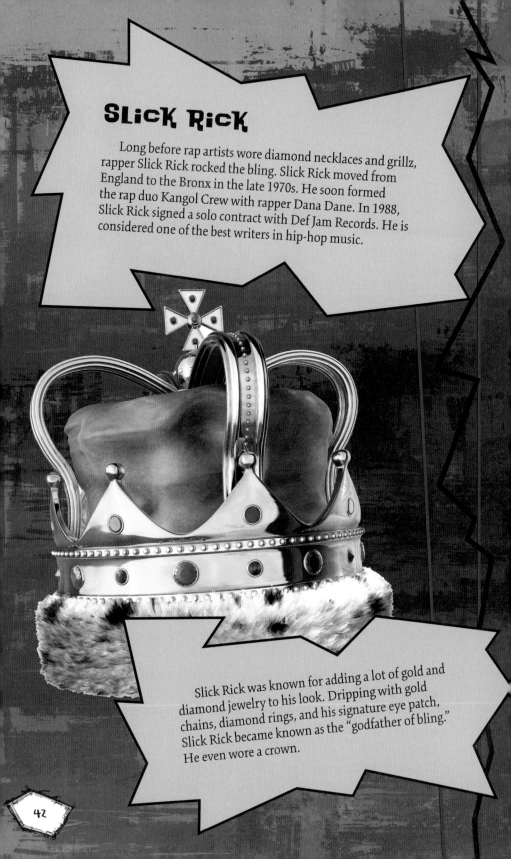

SLICK RICK

Long before rap artists wore diamond necklaces and grillz, rapper Slick Rick rocked the bling. Slick Rick moved from England to the Bronx in the late 1970s. He soon formed the rap duo Kangol Crew with rapper Dana Dane. In 1988, Slick Rick signed a solo contract with Def Jam Records. He is considered one of the best writers in hip-hop music.

Slick Rick was known for adding a lot of gold and diamond jewelry to his look. Dripping with gold chains, diamond rings, and his signature eye patch, Slick Rick became known as the "godfather of bling." He even wore a crown.

» a patch over his right eye

» metal grillz

» large rings

» gold necklaces with huge pendants

Slick Rick always wears an eye patch. As an infant, his right eye was blinded by broken glass in an accident.

ANDRÉ 3000

As a teenager growing up in Atlanta, rapper André 3000 didn't want to dress like everyone else. He dyed his jeans wild colors like blue and orange. In the early 1990s, he formed the hip-hop group OutKast with his high school friend Big Boi. OutKast drew attention for their catchy tunes and André's unique fashion sense.

>> wigs

» golfer hats, straw hats, and fedoras

» ties and bow ties

» preppy vests and sweaters

Best Dressed
In 2005, André 3000 made *Vanity Fair* magazine's International Best-Dressed list.

In 2008, André took his love of fashion to the next level. He started his own fashion line called Benjamin Bixby. The fashions include preppy styles inspired by 1930s college football. André draws the fashion designs himself.

FASHION FORWARD

From the hippie looks of the 1960s to the rocker fashions of the 1970s, music inspires fashion trends. Hip-hop has changed the face of fashion like no other style of music. What began on New York City streets is now in high demand across the globe. From sneakers to jeans to jewelry, hip-hop fashion will continue to shape the way people dress.

GLOSSARY

asymmetrical (ay-suh-ME-tri-kuhl) — a shape that cannot be divided so both pieces match exactly in shape and size

bling (BLING) — flashy jewelry sometimes worn to show wealth

borough (BUHR-oh) — one of the five divisions of New York City, each of which is also a county

breakdance (BRAYK-danss) — a form of street dance that features footwork, floor work, and acrobatic moves

DJ (DEE-jay) — a person who plays pre-recorded music for a radio, party, or club audience

endorse (in-DORS) — to sponsor a product by appearing in advertisements

exhibit (ig-ZI-buht) — a display that shows something to the public

graffiti (gruh-FEE-tee) — letters or pictures painted, scratched, or marked onto a piece of public property

heritage (HER-uh-tij) — history and traditions handed down from the past

MC (em-SEE) — a person who rhymes to the DJ's mix, connecting with the audience in a performance

platinum (PLAT-uh-nuhm) — a very valuable silver-white metal often used in jewelry

preppy (PREP-ee) — a style of dress made up of classic clothing and a neat appearance

rebellious (ri-BEL-yuhss) — disobedience to the people in charge

turntable (TURN-tay-buhl) — a circular, revolving surface used for playing phonograph records

READ MORE

Cornish, Melanie J. *The History of Hip Hop*. Crabtree Contact. New York: Crabtree Publishing, 2009.

Garofoli, Wendy. *Hip-Hop History*. Hip-Hop World. Mankato, Minn.: Capstone Press, 2010.

Jones, Jen. *Fashion History: Looking Great through the Ages*. The World of Fashion. Mankato, Minn.: Capstone Press, 2007.

Thompson, Lisa. *Trendsetter: Have You Got What It Takes to be a Fashion Designer?* On the Job. Minneapolis: Compass Point Books, 2008.

INTERNET SITES

FactHound offers a safe, fun way to find Internet sites related to this book. All of the sites on FactHound have been researched by our staff.

Here's all you do:

Visit *www.facthound.com*

FactHound will fetch the best sites for you!

INDEX